Dothead

Dothead

POEMS

AMIT MAJMUDAR

ALFRED A. KNOPF   NEW YORK   2016

THIS IS A BORZOI BOOK
PUBLISHED BY ALFRED A. KNOPF

Library of Congress Cataloging-in-Publication Data
Majmudar, Amit.
[Poems. Selections]
Dothead : poems / Amit Majmudar.—First edition.
pages cm
ISBN 978-1-101-94707-4 (hardcover)—ISBN 978-1-101-94708-1 (eBook)
I. Title.
PS3613.A3536A6 2016
811'.6—DC23   2015020310

Jacket design by Oliver Munday

Manufactured in the United States of America
First Edition

It is fun to have fun
But you have to know how.

—Dr. Seuss

inscription qui y estoit attachée, et disant que c'estoit une lettre du Grand Seigneur. . . ."—*Journal d'Ant. Galland,* ii. 94.

KAUL, s. Hind. *Kāl,* properly 'Time,' then a period, death, and popularly the visitation of famine. Under this word we read :

1808.—"Scarcity, and the scourge of civil war, embittered the Mahratta nation in A.D. 1804, of whom many emigrants were supported by the justice and generosity of neighbouring powers, and (a large number) were relieved in their own capital by the charitable contributions of the English at Bombay alone. This and opening of Hospitals for the sick and starving, within the British settlements, were gratefully told to the writer afterwards by many Mahrattas in the heart, and from distant parts, of their own country."—*R. Drummond, Illustrations,* &c.

KAUNTA, CAUNTA, s. This word, Mahr. and Guz. *kāntha,* 'coast or margin,' [Skt. *kantha,* 'immediate proximity,' *kanthī,* 'the neck,'] is used in the northern part of the Bombay Presidency in composition to form several popular geographical terms, as *Mahi Kānthā,* for a group of small States on the banks of the Mahi River ; *Rewā Kānthā,* south of the above ; *Sindhu Kānthā,* the Indus Delta, &c. The word is no doubt the same which we find in Ptolemy for the Gulf of Kachh, Κάνθι κόλπος. Kānthī-Kot was formerly an important place in Eastern Kachh, and *Kānthī* was the name of the southern coast district (see *Ritter,* vi. 1038).

KEBULEE. (See **MYROBOLANS**.)

KEDDAH, s. Hind. *Khedā (khednā,* 'to chase,' from Skt. *ākheta,* 'hunting'). The term used in Bengal for the enclosure constructed to entrap elephants. [The system of hunting elephants by making a trench round a space and enticing the wild animals by means of tame decoys is described by Arrian, *Indika,* 13.] (See **CORRAL**.)

[c. 1590. — "There are several modes of hunting elephants. 1. k'hedah" (then follows a description).—*Āīn,* i. 284.]

1780-90.—"The party on the plain below have, during this interval, been completely occupied in forming the **Keddah** or enclosure."—*Lives of the Lindsays,* iii. 191.

1810. — "A trap called a **Keddah**." — *Williamson, V. M.* ii. 436.

1860.—"The custom in Bengal is to construct a strong enclosure (called a **Keddah**

in the heart of the forest." — *Tennent's Ceylon,* ii. 342.

KEDGEREE, KITCHERY, s. Hind. *khichrī,* a mess of rice, cooked with butter and *dāl* (see **DHALL**), and flavoured with a little spice, shred onion, and the like ; a common dish all over India, and often served at Anglo-Indian breakfast tables, in which very old precedent is followed, as the first quotation shows. The word appears to have been applied metaphorically to mixtures of sundry kinds (see *Fryer,* below), and also to mixt jargon or *lingua franca.* In England we find the word is often applied to a mess of re-cooked fish, served for breakfast ; but this is inaccurate. Fish is frequently eaten *with kedgeree,* but is no part of it. ["Fish *Kitcherie*" is an old Anglo-Indian dish, see the recipe in *Riddell, Indian Domestic Economy,* p. 437.]

c. 1340.—"The munj (**Moong**) is boiled with rice, and then buttered and eaten. This is what they call **Kishrī**, and on this dish they breakfast every day."—*Ibn Batuta,* iii. 131.

c. 1443.—"The elephants of the palace are fed upon **Kitchri**."—*Abdurrazzāk,* in *India in XVth Cent.* 27.

c. 1475.—"Horses are fed on pease ; also on **Kichiris**, boiled with sugar and oil ; and early in the morning they get *shishenivo*" (?).—*Athan. Nikitin,* in *do.,* p. 10.

The following recipe for **Kedgeree** is by Abu'l Fazl :—

c. 1590.—"**Khichri**, Rice, split *dāl,* and *ghi,* 5 *ser* of each ; ⅓ *ser* salt ; this gives 7 dishes."—*Āīn,* i. 59.

1648.—"Their daily gains are very small, . . . and with these they fill their hungry bellies with a certain food called **Kitserye**."—*Van Twist,* 57.

1653.—"**Kicheri** est vne sorte de legume dont les Indiens se nourrissent ordinairement."—*De la Boullaye-le-Gouz,* ed. 1657, p. 545.

1672.—Baldaeus has **Kitzery**, Tavernier **Quicheri** [ed. *Ball,* i. 282, 391].

1673.—"The Diet of this Sort of People admits not of great Variety or Cost, their delightfullest Food being only **Cutcherry** a sort of Pulse and Rice mixed together, and boiled in Butter, with which they grow fat."—*Fryer,* 81.

Again, speaking of pearls in the Persian Gulf, he says : "Whatever is of any Value is very dear. Here is a great Plenty of what they call **Ketchery**, a mixture of all together, or Refuse of Rough, Yellow, and Unequal, which they sell by Bushels to the Russians."—*Ibid.* 320.

KEDGEREE INGREDIENTS

Dothead

Well yes, I said, my mother wears a dot.
I know they said "third eye" in class, but it's not
an *eye* eye, not like that. It's not some freak
third eye that opens on your forehead like
on some Chernobyl baby. What it means
is, what it's *showing* is, there's this unseen
eye, on the inside. And she's marking it.
It's how the X that says where treasure's at
is not the treasure, but as good as treasure.—
All right. What I said wasn't half so measured.
In fact, I didn't say a thing. Their laughter
had made my mouth go dry. Lunch was after
World History; that week was India—myths,
caste system, suttee, all the Greatest Hits.
The white kids I was sitting with were friends,
at least as I defined a friend back then.
So wait, said Nick, does *your* mom wear a dot?
I nodded, and I caught a smirk on Todd—
She wear it to the shower? And to bed?—
while Jesse sucked his chocolate milk and Brad
was getting ready for another stab.
I said, Hand me that ketchup packet there.
And Nick said, What? I snatched it, twitched the tear,
and squeezed a dollop on my thumb and worked
circles till the red planet entered the house of war
and on my forehead for the world to see
my third eye burned those schoolboys in their seats,
their flesh in little puddles underneath,
pale pools where Nataraja cooled his feet.

I stood for twenty years a chess piece in Córdoba, the black rook.

I was a parrot fed melon seeds by the eleventh caliph.

I sparked to life in a Damascus forge, no bigger than my own pupil.

I was the mosquito whose malarial kiss conquered Alexander.

I bound books in Bukhara, burned them in Balkh.

In my four hundred and sixteenth year I came to Qom.

I tasted Paradise early as an ant in the sugar bin of Mehmet Pasha's chief chef.

I was a Hindu slave stonemason who built the Blue Mosque without believing.

I rode as a louse under Burton's turban when he sneaked into Mecca.

I butchered halal in Jalalabad.

I had been a vulture just ten years when I looked down and saw Karbala set for me like a table.

I walked that lush Hafiz home and held his head while he puked.

I was one of those four palm trees smart-bomb-shaken behind the reporter's khaki vest.

I threw out the English-language newspaper that went on to hide the roadside bomb.

The nails in which were taken from my brother's coffin.

My sister's widowing sighed sand in a thousand Kalashnikovs.

I buzzed by a tube light, and three intelligence officers, magazines rolled, hunted me in vain.

Here I am at last, born in a city whose name, on General Elphinstone's 1842 map, was misspelt "Heart."

A mullah for a mauled age, a Muslim whose memory goes back farther than the Balfour Declaration.

You may remember me as the grandfather who guided the gaze of a six-year-old Omar Khayyám to the constellations.

Also maybe as the inmate of a Cairo jail who took the top bunk and shouted down at Sayyid Qutb to please please please shut up.

Off with the wristwatch, the Reeboks, the belt.
       My laptop's in a bin.
I dig out the keys from my jeans and do
       my best Midwestern grin.
At O'Hare, at Atlanta, at Dallas/Fort Worth,
       it happens every trip,
at LaGuardia, Logan, and Washington Dulles,
       the customary strip
is never enough for a young brown male
       whose name comes up at random.
Lest the randomness of it be doubted, observe
       how Myrtle's searched in tandem,
how Doris's six-pack of Boost has been seized
       and Ethel gets the wand.
How polite of the screeners to sham paranoia
       when what they really want
is to pick out the swarthiest, scruffiest of us
       and pat us top to toe,
my fellow Ahmeds and my alien Alis,
       Mohammed alias Mo—
my buddies from med school, my doubles partners,
       my dark unshaven brothers
whose names overlap with the crazies and God fiends,
       ourselves the goateed other.

Hell-raiser, razor-feathered
riser, windhover over
Peshawar,

power's
joystick-blithe
thousand-mile scythe,

proxy executioner's
proxy ax
pinged by a proxy server,

winged victory,
pilot cipher
unburdened by aught

but fuel and bombs,
fool of God, savage
idiot savant

sucking your benumbed
trigger-finger
gamer's thumb

My father before me, the watchmaker of Herat, used his monocle and gear
    tweezers to pick a splinter from my ring finger.
Egypt (not Qutb's, Tut's) believed this finger bore a vein that drained
    directly to the heart.
My father's father before him had irises a Bactrian hazel, dating back to the
    third century B.C.
They are the eyes of an ancient rapist who traveled here with Alexander's
    army; but they are the only keepsakes I have.
His father before him was a mountain man, and came down to Herat only
    once, to trade a horse.
Herat took his horse at knifepoint and gave him the cough that killed him
    and two of his brothers.
His father before him shot two British soldiers with a carbine that liked to
    buck left.
The regiment was all redcoated Highlanders, who brought their bagpipes to
    the Hindu Kush.
His third shot sparked strange in the breech and peppered his face.
His father before him, a decorator of Qur'ans, bandaged his only apprentice's
    eyes.
My ring finger is an inkwell full of royal blood, my language, fired tiles and
    tessellation.
Today I stand outside an electrified fence and watch a gunship's rotors spin
    down.
My generations stand behind me in a row, and the draft sets us spinning in
    place:
Sufi pinwheels, seizing any wind as an excuse for ecstasy.

My grandfather, the last illuminator of Qur'ans in Herat, went blind at fifty-two.

All his life, his brush was forbidden cedar forests, clear-eyed falcons, horses, men—

Any shape that might rival God's first stick figure on the dust jacket of life,

Any doodle with a root, hoof, hand, or frond.

A diacritical dot, the rules went, must not masquerade as a watermelon seed.

An alif must not be reborn as a leaf, nor a laam as a lamb, nor a baa as a sheep.

My grandfather's stained-glass cataracts left his eyes as blue-gray as an Englishman's.

Fingertips ink-black, wick-black where the light had long ago alit

Saw by feel his grandson, his living image.

Indigo infused his lenses, madder red his rosacea.

Those lenses were solid haze, as if a dry nib leeched his inkdrop-pupils

To conjure a border or crosshatch mountains outlaw.

Cataracts are waterfalls: When my father closed his father's eyes,

Thousands of unpenned images, unpent at last,

Thrashed upstream to the breeding waters of his dreams.

When they leathered his arm to the armrest and began
like manicurists in a nail salon
he says that he "retreated" from his hand
until the part of him that dwelt there once was gone
and heard no news from his own outer reaches.
In his memoir of those years, he sketches
the tricks he used, one of which was "vision."
Maybe it's better we present his version:
"I imagined my arm as a slope I had to scale,
shaft of the humerus as smooth as shale
but white like bone and giving way like sand
wherever I set foot. I couldn't stand,
couldn't take a breather, or I'd ride my own
disintegration down and end up on
the shore—which was my hand, my fingernails.
I crested my shoulder, rested on its knoll.
I looked down then and saw the pain as men
charging uphill to where I hid my sense
of pain. At once I stomped a foot to see
the whole arm crack, calve, crash into the sea,
disarticulated, part of me no more.
I did this for the other arm and for
my feet and testicles and eyes until
I found myself on a Pacific atoll
that had no latitude, no longitude.
I built a hut, I scuttled the one canoe.
I saw a sun that weighed a kiloton
and the power cord by which it swung."

We were that raghead family
Catching rainfall in a still.
The old famines had us spooked,
Thirst myths passed on to us sons
By our drunk, teary father,
Smack of rock still on his tongue.

Once he had to bite his tongue,
He told us, so his family
Could drink of him. His father
Didn't have to ask. But still,
He said, you boys are good sons.
Just do my will. And don't speak.

We didn't. Nobody spoke
To us, either, though our tongues
Could parrot, palate the sounds.
Yes. Yes, that was my family,
Awed by leavened bread, turnstiles,
Drinking fountains; my father,

Screaming *Respect your father*
In public; me, who did not speak.
Come dawn we poured out the stills
And prayed in a stranger's tongue
For the health of our family
And the rising of the sun.

Can I be my father's son
Without being my father?
Or am I unfamiliar
Because of the way I speak?
This foreign, farangi tongue
That borrowed some words and stole

The rest, imperial style.
I want to be a good son,
But without biting my tongue.
I'm thinking of my father.
It feels like treason to speak
Publicly of my family.

But is it still a family
When the son cannot speak
The mother tongue of the father?

Day One. Monkey is strapped into chair.

Trainee tonsures Monkey and affixes electrodes.

Introductory lecture regarding alternating and direct current,

Trainee and Monkey at desks, side by side.

Day Two. Basics of cocktail preparation.

Sodium thiopental to win minds, potassium chloride to win hearts.

Pancuronium to cure all.

Mint sprig optional.

Day Three. Trainee straps Monkey into chair.

Trainee shaves the rest of Monkey's body and attaches electrodes,

Then EKG leads.

Lecture on induced current, one coil awakening the charge in another.

Day Four. Trainee is to familiarize himself with pertinent knots:

Falconer's knot, grief knot, hunter's bend.

Killick hitch, axle hitch, slipknot, monkey's fist.

Pity not. Noose.

Day Five. Preliminary killings.

Trainee will set out ant bait in at least five corners.

Visit to lobster tank at local grocery store.

Interactive online tutorial, "Do Primates Feel Pain?"

Day Six. Trainee zips previously shaven Monkey into orange jumpsuit.

With Monkey secure in chair, Trainee makes verbal offer of cigarette and Bible.

Trainee attaches electrodes to Monkey, EKG leads to himself.

Supplementary lecture on circuit breakers.

Day Seven. Historical overview:

Asps hooked onto the breasts of empresses,

Peasants sagging down wooden pikes, pistols handed to Soviet generals.

Crucifixion. The arithmetic of quartering.

Day Eight. Self-assessment module.

After leathering properly dressed Monkey into chair,

Trainee places left hand on switch, right hand on heart,

And waits for Monkey, preoccupied with naked tube light, to meet eyes.

On the terrace of the Presidential Palace you lie glued to the scope for less than an hour before you have to take the shot. Tourist or terrorist: It was always going to be your call.

You are applauded for taking the shot and saving the nation, although you are not allowed to rise off your elbows, the knobs of which have begun to ache. A hand—the same hand that occasionally guides a straw into your mouth—reaches around to pin a medal on your lapel.

You keep watch for another twenty-five years, your elbows flattening into steady stands, when the same terrorist, or maybe the terrorist's son, arrives with a bouquet of flowers and drops it on the site of the original killing.

You take the shot again and watch the paramedics carry off the body before the media can get there. They give your sniper scope another thumbs-up sign; you have done well, as a prompt second medal proves.

You begin to realize that you are profiling the visitors to the Presidential Palace on the crudest criteria: skin tone, nose size, turban or no turban, beard or no beard, a certain innate glower to the eyes. Every twenty-five years, you take another shot at a nearly identical-looking man, never quite wiping out his recalcitrant line. It is as though his terrorist descendants are drawn to memorialize one ancient wrong on the birth of a male child every quarter of a century.

You have over a dozen medals on your lapel. Thanks to you, the nation is sure to last a long time. Still, you wonder whether you identified that first terrorist correctly; whether that first killshot prompted the descendants to become terrorists and necessitated all the subsequent killshots.

At last, forty medals later, the nation safe for a thousand years, the rifle is extricated from your grasp and you are peeled off your perch. The Secret Service wheels you upright into the Presidential Palace, where you join the rows of other snipers who have protected the President for millennia.

A great triumphal chorus blasts from speakers in the four corners of the hall. Your arms, like those of your many predecessors, are frozen in position: one hand curled close, trigger finger pointed almost at your heart; the other flared above your head, cradling the absent barrel, index finger pointed almost at the ceiling. Your jaw is massaged until it lowers.

Now you, too, look like a tenor, singing from the heart.

You, too, are part of the choir.

Michelangelo had the model for *David* pinch a grape with his buttocks.

Surrealism was born when a young Luis Buñuel, peering through a hole into his landlady's
bathroom,

Saw she had "a small tail, with a curl like a pig's."

Caravaggio was a closet Muslim, converted at twenty-three by the Turkish dye merchant

Who supplied a rare brown needed for the Virgin Mary's eyes.

Degas attended his first ballet in order to gawk through binoculars at naked ankles.

Perspective, in the first years of the technique, much like polyphony made European
churchgoers vomit.

"The truly new in art can be identified only by its emetic effect."—Salvador Dalí, 1929.

For Titian to have produced all the paintings ascribed to Titian,

The most conservative estimate is he would have had to have started painting at age 10

And painted at least sixteen hours a day

Every day until his death at age 143.

Monet started out trying to stay inside the lines, then lost his glasses.

Every one of his haystacks contains a single needle, done in silver paint, using a single
horsehair.

Giotto kept a black African assistant who, according to the biographer Giorgio Vasari,

"Sketched out the master's frescos on the church walls, and sometimes completed them as
well."

The blackberries in the Dutch painter Jan van Os's still life

Cause ants to abandon genuine grains of sugar

And head single file for the wall:

Look up "Van Os Ants" on YouTube if you don't believe me.

The Cubist Braque slept with the wife of his most prominent realist detractor

And painted, on her freckled shoulder, a single unshooably micromiraculous fly.

Richer than mother's milk
is half-and-half.
Friends of two minds,
redouble your craft.

Our shelves our hives, our selves
a royal jelly,
may we at Benares and Boston,
Philly and Delhi

collect our birthright nectar.
No swarm our own,
we must be industrious, both
queen and drone.

Being two beings requires
a rage for rigor,
rewritable memory,
hybrid vigor.

English herself is a crossbred
mother mutt,
primly promiscuous
and hot to rut.

Oneness? Pure chimera.
Splendor is spliced.
Make your halves into something
twice your size,

your tongue a hyphen joining
nation to nation.
Recombine, become a thing
of your own creation,

a many-minded mongrel,
the line's renewal,
self-made and twofold,
soul and dual.

Hot pink frosting
on my chocolate-
cupcake noggin,

switched-on lightbulb-
yellow, tulip-
bulb top-heavy

orange, sky-blue,
bruise-blue, navy
thought cloud, darkening:

Any towel,
any shawl will
serve as well to

bind this open
wound atop me,
mark me off as

not quite level-
headed, tops on
any watchlist.

It's Old Glory
that I choose this
time: I pleat her,

sweep her, set her
on my head as
reverently as

any U.S.
M.C. honor
guard triangle

on a coffin.

The downside to rising like this:
How the emphasis shifts from your legs.
They cycle the air at the outset,
then slacken, and finally trail

the torso's relentless flexing.
Disuse for a month or two withers
them into mosquito whiskers,
and then, when it's time to descend to

your fellow men and walk beside them,
you land and buckle in a grand
absurd kerfuffle, the satin tent

of wings collapsing over you,
real earth in the mouth
where ethereal used to whisper.

The comma is comely, the period, peerless,
                but stack them one atop
the other, and I am in love; what I love
                is the end that refuses to stop,
the promise that something will come in a moment
                though the saying seem all said;
a grammatical afterlife, fullness that spills
                past the full stop, not so much dead
as taking a breather, at worst, stunned;
                the sentence regroups and restarts,
its notation bespeaking momentum, its silence
                dividing the beats of a heart;

A last tercet reworked like a last will,
        he'd told me he was writing, feeling well,
                but I found his body turned to face the wall,

no bigger than a child's. Eight years ill,
        he slept with his legs drawn up, a letter L.
                I saw three cards beside his bed and all

his meds, hope's aspirin, the spirit's pill,
        the withered fig tree of his IV pole,
                his white skin withered, too, beyond the pale.

I saw how age can leave the skull a hill
        and the breath a white wind whistling in a hole.
                He awoke when a gurney squealed down the hall.

We spoke. He told me how a poem ticks:
        a clock, a bomb, a heart that's been attacked.
                It felt like medicine to hear him talk,

heart medicine because my heart was sick
        to see another Alexandria sacked,
                Goethe burning, Lowell, Job, Balzac,

and though I told myself that death begins
        the work of stocking all the shelves again,
                I knew this rare edition would be gone.

His room's barbaric, biometric din
        was full of screens that lit up and trilled like dawn
                whenever a heart lead came undone.

For all our neat rhymes, John said, death's a mess.
        A juice cup tipped, bedpans, a bleeding mass.
                It doesn't lack for the lachrymose:

I guess sophistication must regress
        to speech as rusticated as the grass
                where rumination bows its head to graze.

We write, we die, and what we've written dies,
        he said, but damn it those were blessed days
                deciding if a given rhyme would do.

His cuff inflated, and gave out with a sigh
        the same old numbers, nothing more to say.
                To think the heartsblood could be measured so:

systolic, diastolic; waking, dream.
        What use defining rhythms for the drama
                if soul won't put her bare fist through the drum?

Back when I was young, he said, it seemed
        the art and the artful were one and the same,
                no sweeter labor than to do my sums,

to jump the fence and grin around the bit.
        Listen, Amit—that's not what it's about.
                It isn't worth it if it isn't bought

with suffering. The best of us have written

    maybe a dozen lines that tap the root.

        The rest? Bout-rimes with dead men, overwrought.

I sensed the disappointment in him, the fear.

    But John, I told him, beauty is a fire

        those who burn hardest labor coldly for

and I for one will hold your labors dear,

    the music of meaning, the artistry that dares

        to conjure walls that it might conjure doors.

His twin has lost another tooth today.
　　I try not to make too big a to-do.
　　　　Tomorrow, two more Easter eggs to dye

for coming into, coming back to life,
　　my heart prayed out with gratitude he lived.
　　　　He's elfin-eared and easier to lift,

my boy, my boy who isn't going to grow,
　　born with a holey heart, his lips blue-gray,
　　　　his body shivering at seven degrees

inside a baby greenhouse all for him,
　　his life support a lullaby-like hum
　　　　for the month and a half we couldn't take him home,

that cruel April of a risen sun
　　and a second sun that almost set too soon,
　　　　drawn from the wound-dark sea in a seine.

Son, you are perfect, your arms and legs are perfect,
　　the knees and knobs and nose of you are perfect,
　　　　sealed septum, welded breastbone, perfect, perfect,

precisely the size and sorcery you are:
　　beyond a surgeon's, poet's, father's art
　　　　this sprung rhythm of your spring-risen heart.

Fe

Wealth is a wolf, in the hedge found.
She eyes you, blinking cold coins.

Ur

The aurochs, Thor's ur-ox,
Rushes the hunter in his camo vest.

Thur

The workweek is a ladder of thorns
We ascend to the rose of a weekend.

Os

The ash tree blossomed these runes.
Awestruck, we are most us.

Rad

Riding is sacred, asphalt a psalm.
Hells Angels read the road.

Kaun

Contagion, bedbound, keeps count
As fever's red creeps up five.

Hagall

Hail falls on the desert, a cold seed.
White wheat halos all the hills.

Nyd

Need knits his brows over his bills.
How does a have-not have three jobs?

Isa

Ice is deceiving, glass on the lake.
It chokes children without a trace.

Ar

Earth is an heiress rumored rich,
Left a legacy of acrid air.

Sol

The sun, unsullied, smiles dully
At the soiled creek, the spilling oil.

Tyr

Tired of war, we wear our tears,
Interior amulets.

Bjarkan

We bark at the sky as hard as we can,
But the gods remain swingers of birches.

Maor

The more he wants no more than he has,
The more he becomes more than he is.

Logr

Bottoms up in the name of the father,
Water of life or bitter lager.

Yr

A new yew erupts from Ur's sewers.
Time eats its young and rewrites the ruins.

Hrhm Shp, colt-culling,
Is what hoof lore calls it—
The choke-chain sound a roan coined
To describe the things he saw
Before the sniff weevils crept
Up his nostrils and chewed
His eyes at the hue-sweet root.

•

Mother mares scare foals
From folly-trots and foxglove
By telling them fury tales
Of muck stirrup-deep and shells
Shoveling Passchendaele
Onto Passchendaele,
The foal fallen with the boy.

•

One memory, common
To all breeds, spurs night mares
Sparking down the mute streets
Of their sleep, gas-blind
Witnesses scraping Krupp

Guns over the cobblestones,
Winged sparks breeding in the hay.

•

Having watched us box and ditch
Our dead, they thought our dead
Ate termite-runnels
In the black bark of the land
And pulled all horsefolk down
To join whatever dark cavalry
Thundered underground.

•

The burlap gas mask cupped
And strapped to the wet snout
Could be mistaken, when
The gas gong sounded
And the men grew fly-heads,
For a feed sack chock-
Full of red ants.

ADAM

The only proof we have of intelligent design is that Adam could not connect his mouth and his penis. His designer was so aware of the risk that he designed Adam with a two-rib buffer. One rib eventually went to make Eve, but the second made sure Adam never lost interest in her. If given the ability to fellate himself, he would have poured himself endlessly into himself, like an ocean evaporating into one fixed cloud and raining on its own waves, greening nothing. The act would have been a means to knowing himself biblically—to self-knowledge—and as such would have vaulted Adam above the sexless archangels. He might well have lost interest in God, too, bowing only to himself, rising a little, bowing again. Eve and Eden would have blossomed, Satan would have hissed in vain as Adam rocked like a pill bug on the grass, our species committing suicide as its intended first parent over and over again shot himself in the head.

BREATH

Between the nose and the throat, we swallow in the same place we breathe. The pharynx is an anteroom where breath and drink mingle before they are sent, by the mindless knowingness of the body, down their separate tunnels. The breath is constantly blowing up and down, just beyond, while the head continues its own up-and-down, the life-giving movement crosswise to the pleasure-giving one. The ancients believed that God blew the breath of life, the *nishmat chayim*, into a mud effigy. In this sense, the arousal of Adam to life was the first blow job. The first time my first girlfriend was forced to give one, she kept stopping every ten to fifteen seconds. Holding one thing in her mouth, reflexively she held the other as well. *It's okay,* I told her. *Breathe.*

COME

At the moment you come, the spinal cord detaches from the brain and whips down, forward, and out, liquefying as it leaves you. The dull pearl hue of come comes from mixing gray matter and white matter. Immediately before that moment, gooseflesh prickles up the neuraxis and the body gives a slow, rising shudder—as if a third, colder presence had come into the room and blown, ever so gently, on the naked back. This is the same shudder Eve felt when the serpent came inside the garden: her first adumbration of the female orgasm, courtesy of Lucifer.

DUINO

Duino Elegies, in Edward Snow's translation, sat on the nightstand next to her bed. She had bookmarked it with its own receipt. I kept turning my head to it, pondering its thinness and the thinness of books of poetry generally, and wondering what a *duino* was, and wondering why my head was not in the getting of head when head was what I had wanted for so long. I knew nothing of Rilke then—she introduced me to poetry, too: you'd think we would have kept in touch—but I had seen, maybe on a calendar, the famous quote about how love is two people protecting each other's solitude. At the end, when she rose onto her knees at the foot of the bed, distanced from me by the length of my body, looking to the side, perhaps at that very book on the nightstand, I did feel loneliness. Loneliness is just solitude without a book. *O fig tree, how long I've pondered you . . .*

EYES

When Adam first asked Eve to look up at him, he thought eye contact would be like touch, only deeper. His mind would enter the upper half of her head as his body was entering the lower half of it. She, too, wanted to lock eyes, believing it would connect them—it was getting lonely and tedious down there, and she was wondering whether she preferred the snake-eyed sweetness of the apple to the salty tree sap of Adam. But Adam thought her left eyebrow rose slightly as she looked up, and he couldn't shake an impression of *knowingness*, which only reminded him of their lost innocence. Eve saw him looking down at her from his height and sensed a new hierarchy between them, in which he made demands, and she knelt and serviced him. *Non serviam*, she insisted, but her mouth was full as she said this, and Adam mistook it for a groan of pleasure.

FACE

They couldn't have learned it from watching the beasts of the field. For many—the giraffe, the horse—the logistical barriers to any technique other than mounting are insurmountable. The closest thing they could have witnessed was the mutual investigative sniff between dogs. For that matter, even the default position of human copulation, face-to-face, had little precedent in nature. The new discovery cleared Eve out of Adam's field of view. This transition in his pleasure, from Eve's face to the absence of her face, made the pleasure twice removed from the pleasure of beasts: consummately solitary, consummately human. Before the fall, Adam lay on his back and marveled at clouds and their infinite counterfeit forms. After the fall, he stood and watched himself in a mirror.

GAG

This second fruit—over which Adam had taken to wearing a leaf, creating the illusion he, too, was a tree—seemed as forbidden as the apple, and as such, irresistible. Eve found out how seriously she had transgressed only when, devouring it whole, as a serpent might its noonday meal, she felt an unexpected lurch, her whole neck and torso rising in revolt. She fell back onto her heels, coughing. If only the apple had convulsed her so! Everything might have been different. She would have never swallowed that bite of the forbidden. She would have done nothing more than hold the forbidden in her mouth, like smoke, or a pill, or now, returning onto her knees, Adam.

HEAD

The physical expressions of love are really just people rubbing together the most sensitive parts of their bodies. We rub hands, we rub lips and tongues, we rub genitals because that's where the nerve endings are. We rub them the way paramedics rub defibrillator paddles before delivering the jolt: Well-given head makes the getter arch off the bed, electrified. To get head is to have the lover's thinking head sleeve your unthinking head. Two civilizations at vastly different stages of development are meeting. The thinking head is a cluster of highly developed organs of perception—eyes, ears, nose, tongue—not to mention the neurological capital, where decisions are made. It is the body's technological North. The head of the penis is nothing but nerves, something rudimentary, not yet a mind. This head is capital of a hot-blooded rebel country, hypersensitive and easily roused: the body's humid, tumid South.

INNOCENCE

It seemed like a way of having it both ways, at that age. Pleasure without risk, intimacy without a sinking sense of obligation. You could get your knowledge without having it age you. It should have been playful. I shouldn't have had to put my hands on her shoulders and, ever so gently, press. Because I was everything at once in the garden of my greenness. I was innocent Adam and insidious Lucifer. I was also the Tree, the standing wood of life, coaxing an Eve curious but full of foreboding, *Taste of me. Taste of me.*

JOB

Blowing Adam became one of the many jobs of Eve's exile, the milking of one more udder. Repetition: Cain the infant, Abel the toddler loved it. Their minds still carried an amniotic glisten of innocence, which wouldn't rub off until their teens. Repetition, though, their mother could not bear. In Eden, things had been different: twelve hours of daylight, twelve of dark, the saying of the same prayers at the same times of day, the three hungers and the three meals, Eve's nightly up down up down up down until Adam spouted like Old Faithful on a seismic timer—in Eden all this retained delight, every time, the same way the same story told the same way delighted the children: In the beginning was the word, once upon a time. In exile, boredom became possible. Music was the only language that could take them back, please them with repetition—though now even songs, they realized, could age. Repetition: Within a few years, Eve and Adam stopped speaking in verse. They longed for a new rhythm from moment to moment, which is the same thing as longing for no rhythm at all. The language of knowledge has always been prose.

KISS

She placed her affection, almost daintily, on the feverish forehead of lust. I wanted to inspire awe, like some dark alien obelisk discovered in the jungle: I wanted to be jaw-dropping. But here were kisses, gentle ones, kisses I had never asked for, kisses better suited to the cheeks of nephews, kisses that undercut my male aggression like long-stemmed roses slid down a riot gun. Later, when we broke up and the reproaches came out all at once, she told me that she hadn't really wanted to, that I had been pushy, that she had worried she would lose me if she didn't, that she wished she never had. Kisses. I realize now she was buying time.

LUCIFER

Lucifer had no idea, when he decided to take the form of the serpent, how he would move once he was in it. The wingless, footless form seemed a perfect disguise for one who would be expected to enter either gliding or on tiptoe. The trick, once he lay prone on the ticklish grass, was not to lead with his front end, but to squeeze himself from the base to the head. The tongue spilled forward on its own, like toothpaste from a tube. So did the seven ounces of breath that composed his hiss.

MNMMN

To give pleasure the mouth sacrifices speech. The conversation across the table that
gave way to whispering on the futon gave way, at last, to silence. I did not speak
because, for me, four months' speaking had attained its goal. I had listened, too, listened
always with this future silence in mind, though it seems calculating to accuse a boy that
young of such calculation, even if the accuser and the accused are me and me. She tried
to speak once, that first time, a couple syllables, or maybe one syllable that struggled
twice to emerge. Everything comes out sounding the same, this *mnmmn* that is neither
moan nor murmur. She could have been saying yes, or baby, or more, or Amit, or oh,
or (we were both so young, we were boy and girl) no.

NO

It wouldn't have taken much. If she had said the word, I would have sucked myself back
like a touch-me-not, touched. No means no, we were taught in Health class. No means
no, said the Sex Ed VHS on the television our teacher wheeled into the classroom.
No one ever taught us what silence meant. Silence means whatever the person not
listening wants silence to mean. And I wanted hers to mean yes that afternoon between
Rilke's elegies and the rest of summer break. The second time, the third time, all the
other times, she told me later, I wanted to. Just not that first time. And I, guilty, all I could
do was murmur: I didn't know, I didn't know, I didn't know.

O

O opens any ode. It is the default orison sung by heavenly choristers, the only letter
that fashions the mouth in its own image, the original rabbit hole of the original fall:
Out of Eden, into Wonderland. In the room where I was first blown, a ceiling punkah

turned furiously in the humid heat, and I stared up at its circular blur. It was over only when my mouth rounded itself to match hers and I shouted, loudly once and the second time more softly, in a decrescendo, *O, o.*

PULL

Adam's sensitive hardness had a pull on Eve even before they found out pleasure could divorce itself from pelvis-to-pelvis procreation. Fellatio wasn't just some corrupt, postlapsarian innovation. Before, in her innocence, she went down to learn more about him, the way she bent sometimes to inspect Eden's earthworms and orchids. After the fall, Eve went down to fall farther, to fall all the way, to do nothing of use with the sacred tools of speech and sex. This was the pull toward him, but after the fall, there was also an opposite force at work the other way. Call it resentment. Adam noticed how her going down, quickening toward the finish, flipped its directionality. She wasn't going down anymore—just repeatedly, and tenaciously, pulling away.

QUESTION

That afternoon, for whole minutes before it actually happened, the experience floated just beyond me, a ring of smoke. Asking the question, even leaving off the part that would make the question make sense, *Will you,* would have swished away everything by grasping it. And so I communicated what I wanted with a brush of my finger across her lips, my hands sliding onto her small shoulders, my back arching as I glanced down at myself as though here, between us, were a flesh wound that needed her nursing. It would have felt wrong to speak this want stronger than mere need, this curiosity too intense for questions. She never said no because I never asked.

RHYTHM

Adam's rhythm, standing behind Eve (their first experiments aped the apes), slowed down or speeded up on its own. His mind didn't govern it so much as his pelvis, the anatomy autonomous. Whenever Eve took him in her mouth, though, questions of rhythm—how to set, sustain, modulate it—entered her head. She speeded up toward the climax, mimicking Adam's thrusting tempo, because she knew her endgame was to mimic nature. Before she sensed that tiptoe-tremulous shiver, and sometimes the unwelcome clap of his hands on her ears, she played with what would become meters: dactylic, halfway, halfway, all the way down; iambic, halfway, then down to the base; or Adam's favorite, the emphatic spondee.

SELF-REFLEXIVE

The ouroboros, the serpent sucking on itself, has been the envy of mystics and alchemists for centuries. It represents perfect sufficiency, pleasure given and received in equal measure, a creature that has formed a ring and married itself. One could imagine that ring tightening until the serpent became all head and the jaws everted into pure absence, like a reversible purse whose inner lining was the void. Which serpent appears in this symbol, it doesn't take a leap to imagine. The tempter in the garden must have taunted Eve and Adam, afterward, with this very same now-you-see-me trick, deep-throating himself in an auto-da-fellatio, tasting of the one fruit more forbidden than the apple.

TEETH

Rilke compares the tongue between the teeth to the heart between hammers. And the tongue is covered in nerve endings, sensing, in its cloister, more intensely than other parts of the body. When you place a part of yourself more sensitive than your tongue between someone *else's* teeth, the one who kneels is not the one who surrenders. Any gesture of dominance or control, like the hand on the head that presumes to bless this genuflection, guide this descent, is just for show. The one who isn't biting down is the one in charge. A girl named Nicole once ran our high school football team, and on Monday morning, when everyone knew, I could not detect anything like shame on her used face, only triumph, as though she were a warrior princess, and a rival army one by one had knelt to kiss her sword.

URGENCY

When I was young and could not bear to go slow, when holding hands across a table at Applebee's and even making out felt like salt flats seen from a car going the speed limit, I couldn't taste the dessert we spooned together. It could have been apple pie, it could have been a wedge of wet clay. All the motions of the date took on the feel of running in a dream. When the time came at last, I placed myself in her mouth like a beating donor heart on ice.

VERSAILLES

A garden's a garden only until something grows without permission. No plant is born a weed save in its gardener's eye: What lives must live by design or not at all. Eden, willed wild, was never some Versailles, never some grid of green hallways and foursquare grottoes. Eden had tangled ivies but no weeds until Adam and Eve dared to grow their own minds up. From that moment, they themselves became the first weeds in Eden—detected, dug up, and flung over the wall. By then, a sense of flower and weed governed how they looked at their bodies: hence the fig leaf meant to camouflage Adam's new patch of loosestrife, Eve's coarse triangle of crabgrass. In fact, the flesh stem of his penis itself came to seem a weed—one she could never, for all her kneeling and pulling, uproot.

WOOD

Why not iron, why not marble, why not brass? Because desire, in all the old poems, is supposed to be a flame, and fire swallows wood. Because men, even at their most vulgar, prefer to liken this part of their bodies to something animate, organic: hence boner, hence cock, hence meat. Because wood, back when it was the trunk of a tree, dribbled sticky white sap and coursed at its pith with water. Because the Tree of Life and the Tree of Knowledge had scaffolds, at least, of a common material, and because they were both wood they, too, could burn, could blossom, could rot.

X

A cutting from a fern grows the same fern in a different spot. Simply incubating Adam's rib was not enough. Something had to be changed. Adam's chromosomes were X and Y, Eve's were X and X: a stubby appendage added to her genome, subtracted from her genitals. This zero-sum made all the difference. A body surfaced more finely, better insulated, more flexible—these were revisions made by a practiced hand, a second draft, fewer mistakes and fewer risks. A patient aesthetic came into play, too, flourishes neglected in the first version: an upcurl given to each eyelash, a lighter voice in her throat, a deeper walnut dye for her hair, for her mouth more madder red.

YEARNING

What I wanted: To be held in her mouth like a secret. To be known, but not completely, not yet, not while I was still riding the bus to school every day. To gain knowledge without losing our innocence, or at least not all of our innocence. To do something serious in a way that could be played off as playfulness, afterward. To dip myself into her like a toe into a pool, but safely, in the shallow end, where even if I fell I could find my feet and walk out. To taste sex the way the rich taste wine, treasuring it on the tongue before spitting.

ZZZ

On the last day of their innocence, Adam arched his back and groaned and rested his head on some stones, which in those days had not yet hardened themselves toward man. Eve rose and, wiping her mouth, found him asleep. At this moment, the serpent emerged from a ravine. The serpent knew she would go looking for a stream or fruit tree soon, to get rid of the aftertaste, and he had to intercept her early. Adam had just fallen asleep, so the serpent did not speak with his long serpent tongue. Instead he stuck it out and wagged it side to side, showing Eve what Adam had never yet, in his selfish innocence, done unto her. Eve held her hand out to the serpent, as she often did to geese and jaguars, and the breezy thwips of his tongue concentrated between her first and middle fingers. Unlike the geese, unlike the jaguars, the serpent was neither eating from her hand nor licking it. He did this with his tongue solely to give her a sensation. Eve had never received a gift before. She sat on the grass, a few feet from where Adam snored, to puzzle out her own delight. The serpent, his tongue still out and moving, crawled into her lap.

The one book where we never lose our place
spreads its covers to a gooseflesh Braille.
We are bookmarks slipped into each other.
In that book, we read each night of a couple
who go without touching for hours on end;
then, the dishes put away, the toddler
powered down and set to charge for tomorrow,
they thumb a lock and make a greenhouse
where once there was a master bedroom.
Orchids push open the drawers. Honeybees
bother the reading lamp.
The carpet threads itself with grass
twitching higher in a sunset-sunrise time-lapse
as the house regresses to a forest,
the plumbing to brooks, the chandeliers to stars,
and "mommy" and "daddy" to the first lovers ever
under a glazed glass dome the size of the sky,
no duty save sensation,
the scar from her Cesarean
his Tropic of Capricorn. At last the throbbing
vines that roped them flush to the bed
slink back into the box spring.
The greenhouse shatters into mist
to reveal a plaster ceiling. They pull apart,
fall open like the covers of a book,
their years together pressed, preserved,
petals they can place on their tongues.

A naked woman

used to be sacred, once.

A woman clothed in nothing

but her own words (and what words, Anne,

what words)

is beyond naked: is transparent.

I stare at photographs online sometimes

and try to peer through

the Delphic chasm, the sibylline leaf of you.

I have aborted poetry like yours in the womb

simply by prescribing lithium.

Every time I wonder, am I killing Anne

by keeping Anne

from killing Anne?

If you were alive today, I might have been your shrink.

Framed diploma, Freudian sangfroid.

I like to think

I would have dropped my prescription pad

and kissed your right hand from the knuckles

around to the life line and out to the nicotine fingertips.

But I am flattering myself.

In real life, I'm scared of heights

and open flames

and women poets. One does not marry

a precipice. One does not have a daughter

with a spiked blue crown of natural gas.

And women who live as fire falling

endlessly from the sky

tend to fall in with hurricanes.

Aeneas looks on piously
while the Sibyl moans and the god mounts her.
You deserved a religion of goddesses,
priestesses, talking birds.
What you got was diagnosed.
I'm no hurricane, I'm a worrywart, Anne,
I'm the shy heart with the side part, Anne,
too scared to ride in your stationary car.
On what blue coast did you coast to a stop?
What song was on the radio?
And when your irises turned into seas
did you strip off your dress and swim?

We weren't born to live
long among the cracked
homes and crack
houses of the real.
Basketball court
fault lines smoke
with dandelion clocks,
something volcanic
in this city's decay.
Car alarms sing
across widowed lots,
and in rushes the sea.
Baby, be good to me.

We weren't born to live
long drinking the tap water
zinc, the expired
milk of the real.
We must grow our hearts up
in this hothouse
of broken windows
because our bodies
have grown up by themselves.
Vets nest
in the hollows of buildings,
and in rushes the sea.
Baby, be good to me.

ot.

ice

rs

eyes,

Pebble-plated
noir and olive
with a palm-pale
flip side, she is
lying sly, her
brow an eyelid-
fitted islet
in the knee-high
Nile shallows.
Ever since the
Eocene, the
scene has hardly
altered; love re-
quires all its
stubby-leggèd
snaggle-toothèd
devotees to
dance a two-step.
Now his heavy-
breathing maw is
moving in an
antediluvian
heavy petting.
He is gently
agile in his
next maneuver,
getting her at
last cloaca
to cloaca:

Linked, they sink in
zodiac-a-
ligned and kissing-
kismet genome-
swap, two uglies
bumping uglies,
age-old algae-
covered lovers
going under
in a fade-out
swirl of delta
silt and bubbles.

Let the hunchback lie hump down
upon the Bactrian camel. On that snug foundation
let the leper stand tiptoe, balancing
the cripple's cane on his nose, while the cripple,
upside down, balances atop the cane, index finger
on the hook handle. Let the cripple's legs scissor
and interlock with the gymnast's, whose chalked hands
should support the flat-footed orangutan.
Let the orangutan be trained beforehand
to hold a dead veteran overhead, the body draped.
On the veteran's shoulders and hips let the retiree
align the rubber-nubbin feet of his walker
and, standing tall, wear a hard hat with a flagpole
coming off it, atop that flagpole a circus elephant,
one leathery foot planted, the body rocking back.
On the top curve of that elephant's S-shaped trunk
let the seal lie arching its back, on its whiskery snout
a beach ball that looks like a globe, spinning.
Let the five-star general clap his hands on that beach ball.
You know he wants to. Let him do a handstand on it.
Feet on his feet, let the poet turning clockwise
support a fruit bat on his head, and let that fruit bat
in turn support a larger fruit bat, between whose ears
should rest the toe of the ballerina's vertical left shoe.
Let the ballerina hold the stepladder steady.
At this point, the tower will have crossed the cloud cover;

the shelf should be in view, and what is kept upon the shelf.
Now let the child skip school. Let the child
climb the tower to its tippy top and place her hand
inside the jar and bring the cookies to earth.

I had

one with

a spiral

painted

on it that

drilled the

coffee

table

when I

spun it.

I'd snap

a die

onto its

blunted corner and watch the twist I gave

it blur the cube into a 3-D Star of David—

my first magic trick, Newtonian hocus-pocus.

A top survives by narrowing its focus: The more

its point attempts to circumscribe, the broader the

circle its handle describes. Waver falls to wobble,

wobble falls to fall. Tightness of any kind at all

leaves room for no love but the discipline.

It lets in less and less and less.

A figure skater, crouching

for the spin, gathers

no one to his

chest.

Every tripod-
toting birder
knows it never
nests on urban

girders. Even
fences set its
scalded-crimson
head askew, its

waddle swinging,
wings akimbo.
Few have got it
on their lists and

fewer still have
caught it singing,
this endangered
North American

candor, cousin
of the done-in
dodo, big-eyed
Big Sur tremor-

tenor—only
ten or twenty
hang glide over
Modoc County,

humbly numbered
(as their days are)
for us crazy
crown- and throat- and

belly-gazers.
Any niche as
fragile as a
candor's renders

its extinction
certain. We can
sabotage its
habitat with

half a laugh or
quarter murmur,
fluster coveys'
worth of candors

off their branches,
which, abandoned,
soon are little
more than snarking-

grounds for minor
birds, the common
snipe, the yellow-
bellied bittern.

When money changes hands
The fingers morph
Into digits. Your changed
Hands grow slowly
More grasping, their once-
Fine arts increasingly
Sketchy. Even a handshake
Takes the measure
Of a stranger's worth.
Your hands, once changed
By money, never do
Change back, hardened
And sharpened, knuckles
Turned to nickel, cuticles
Tipped with nails. Every
Morning, your left handcuffs
Itself by a Bulova
To a speeding commuter train.
The change spares
Your wrists at first, but in time
It plaques on up your arms
Like green on copper
Or ivy up a league.
By tax season, anything
An unseen hand can bundle
Is a fund, anything
In reach is a rung.
Your hands are nothing if not
Climbers, and the high

Is worth it, there on a ledge
Seventy-five stories
Above New York, the usual
Empty hands pointing up
While yours, in answer, raise
Like two feelers
On a metamorphosis
Your long unfeeling
Middle fingers.

And Flintlock begat Springfield, the breech birth,
And Springfield begat Enfield, and Enfield begat Gatling,
And Gatling begat Maxim, who begat Rat, who begat
The blessed Twin boys Tat and Tat,
And Tat begat Kalashnikov, who begat Kalashnikov, Kalashnikov,
        Kalashnikov, Kalashnikov.

To make yourself a dum-dum bullet
That will on impact rip apart,
That when you shoot somebody's stomach
Will lodge a fragment in his heart,
I recommend this simple method,
It's quick, and quite low-cost,
Just take a switchblade to your bullet
And carve a little cross.

Messrs. Smith & Wesson, little one,
Are here to share a lesson, little one,
Never walk to school alone,
Always bring your piece along.
O piece, O piece, O piece on earth,
O piece in which all men exult,
The silly girls want pretty ponies,
The smart ones want a Colt.

Pop-pop-pop quiz, facts are facts.
Forget your reading: Add, subtract.
Arithmetic admits no sentiment.
Sixth Commandment, Second Amendment.

And Winchester begat Remington, and Heckler begat Koch,
And Walther, son of Luger, begat Glock upon Beretta,
And their lineage spread across the earth, to the shooting-range
Appalachians, to Stockton in its hoodie, to the camo-vested Dakotas,
Yea, unto the kindergartens of furthest Connecticut
Their children and their children's children spread,
The automatic and the semiautomatic, the all-American equalizer,
The sawed-off, the cocked, the locked and loaded manstopper, childstopper,
For such was the will of God, the granddaddy of all Founding Fathers.

John Moses Browning, born in Ogden, Utah,
Took, in his smithy, the measure of men.

Nine millimeters, end to end.

Observe the Argive,
        redivivus
with his Bethesda
        Special prosthetic
elbows, his Versed-
        reversed remember-
remember, looking
        alive in olive—
the aftershave
        civilian, the crew-cut
oorah. His stop-
        loss odyssey
went Kabul, morphine,
        Ramstein, Stateside,
and back—round-robin
        desert wrestling,
tag out, tag in.
        Now, retrofitted,
the soon-to-be
        robohobo
thumps down the Jetway,
        a glint in his eye,
springs in his step,
        no place like home.

Because I could *eat.*

I could eat a horse, but my girlfriend wants me to cut back on meat.

I could eat this office building, all umpteen floors of it, cubicles, struts, and caulking.

I could spoon Osiris out of the river Nile and wash him down with the blood of Richard
  Dawkins.

I could simmer khmer in a pol pot and still have room for kim jong-il with rooster sauce.

I could snatch the Lean Cuisine from the beeping microwave of my boss's boss's boss.

I could wolf down a vampire and sink my teeth in a zombie's neck.

I could pick off stars like chicken feed with a peck peck peck peck peck.

I could go for a Russian sub right now and savor its nukes like so much pepper.

I could gut a thousand laser printers and feed my yawning maw their paper.

I'm kind of hankering for the dark matter at the galaxy's gooey core.

I could detach my mandible and swallow until my midriff matched the skyline of New York.

I could shred the Great Plains and the Ukraine alike, a one-man locust swarm.

I could s'more the marshmallow moon on a stick until it's droopy warm.

Seven spheres my caviar, seven seas my primordial soup of the day,

I jones for the bread bowl, the surf and the turf, the Prime Rib and shrimp tray,

The succulent, truculent hurricane, the delicacy of its eye,

The three worlds, the four winds, the pastrami and the rye.

Lot's wife looked back and froze to salt. I look up and burn to sugar.
My master's ashes swirl worlds. His chalk dust turns to sugar.

I'm all sweet tooth and golden tongue but still can't say your Name.
Water is life, granted, but Lord I sure yearn for sugar.

Stir into the sky, dissolve, let your atoms sweeten the rain.
Ashes, ashes, we all fall down. You alone return to sugar.

Beauty, like birth, takes labor. Be rule-bound, but be game.
How much salt must a lover sweat to earn his sugar?

                              Spurn that dirty sugar. Indulgence decays.
                              Most of you is water. What remains is salt.

                              Bitter is best. Sour surely deserves praise.
                              If you can't stomach these, better aim for salt.

                              No sweet-talking Judgment, Amit, come the end of days.
                              Just you wait. Your honeyed words will sound the same as salt.

No weed's a weed but in
            its gardener's eye
forever seeing otherwise.
            This is the same
dissatisfaction that
            deemed even Adam
an unbecoming growth
            and wedded both
to seed and spade, to breed
            and birth in blood.
A gardener whose vision
            is keen enough
can see a weed in any
            deviance of green.
And this is why I fear
            Utopians
and everybody in
            the business of
perfecting out of love
            the world we have—
these gardeners of men.
            You can't foresee
before they come to power
            who's going to be
the weed and who the flower.

Asquith had it from Haldane,
Who had it from Poincaré,
While Viviani's tête-à-tête
At tea with Edward Grey
Revealed that Bethmann cabled
Paléologue to say
The very thing Sazonov said
To Moltke's attaché.

I see London,
I see France,
I see Clio's
Underpants:
Muse of History,
Muse of the Meuse,
Pardon my French,
But Muse, *j'accuse*.

It's time for the name game, children, the blame game.
Come get your clues. Now what begins with B?
Beginnings, Baghdad, Balfour, Bosch, Berlin, let's see:
It's time for the name game, children, the same game
That launched a thousand dreadnoughts
That launched a thousand dead men on the oil-dark sea.

The innominate equal the innumerable.
Statisticians do their Sommes,
But the nom de guerre and the nom de plume
Leave all but the scholars numb.

Remarque, Barbusse, Sassoon, and Graves
Saw through a sniper scope
Their future lines, as fine as crosshairs
Trained on the Death of Hope—
Surely an epic theme, in time,
Source of their deathless fame.
Collar a scholar, you find a schoolboy
Out to make his name.

Joffre muttered to Lanrezac
During the "Marseillaise"
The same thing Falkenhayn confided
To Ludendorff the day
Kitchener cabled French what Haig
Was told without delay,
Rational actors, learning their lines
For Passchendaele's Passion play.

The names, the names, the names remain,
These letters, nailed in place,
Though soldiers down in the soiled earth
Though Tommies drowned in the solid earth
Vanished without a

Marnefully sobbing, hiccuping Ypres Ypres,
The mum of the lad (she, unidentified; he, unidentifiable)
Expects no Clemenceau from stern War.
A nor'waster pulls into the Gare de L'Waste.
Don't worry, O generic Mum-of-Lad, O mute
Liverpudlian Hecuba in your unisex ankle-length
Gabardine coat: Bad news has Gavrilo Princip aim.
The War Office telegram will target you by name.

Laudanum-lullabied, schnapps-
Nightcapped, hemophiliac
Kings and hot-blooded counselors
Sit up in bed with chest pains,
But when the doctors arrive,
Stethoscopes out, to listen,
Each unbuttoned silk nightshirt
Reveals the crisp soot print of
     A black hand.

Gavrilo Princip's standing
On the wrong street this June day
With his hands in his pockets
When the archduke's open-top
Car takes a right turn and stops.
Gabriel feels a soft throb,
Looks down, and sees to his shock
There, at the end of his arm,
     A black hand.

Charcoal on the cheeks is best
For night raids gathering fresh-
Blown roses off a thornbush.
In a land that is no man's
Lies a man that is no man,
His helmet glowing yellow-
Green then going out again—
A firefly cupped in night's
     Black hands.

Kindest of all: the Harlem
Hellfighters. *Ich black slave, du*
White slave, they chuckle, poking
A cigarette in a near-
Dead Bosch's mouth as if he were
A new dad. Yet in this hell
They bring hell, give hell, and close
The black eyes of their black dead
        With black hands.

1. *The Astronomy of Bond Girls*

I want to name stars the way Ian Fleming named women.

Every falling star a Domino Vitali,
The star of Bethlehem rechristened Vesper Lynd,
The polestar reliably Moneypenny.

Bodies celestial deserve such invention,
And not just the stars, the blonde comets, too.
Name one for Honey Rider coming
Again and again, almost the same gold
As Botticelli's Ursula Undress
Holding her own seashell on Crab Kythera.

Imagine our own lonely Sol
Stripped bare
Letting us in on her full name,

Solitaire,

And the implacable black hole
At our galaxy's core
Pussy Galore.

2. *The Short and Happy Life of Plenty O'Toole*

This one died in golden paint,
Fleshious metal, trophy blonde.

This one splashed among piranhas.
This one, while she danced with Bond,

Swung in his arms as a pistol rose,
Took the bullet, and took a dip.
This one licked some poison dripped
Down a thread onto her lip.

This one suffered death by hammock,
Strangled in its rope cocoon.
This one drowned herself in Venice,
The only one who died too soon.

How much better so to perish,
Well before the next year's film;
Not to move into his flat,
Wipe his sink, or cook for him;

Mix the drink, then see him irked you
Served him his martini stirred.
Even worse, for all the jam he
Wipes on his pajama shirt,

Old man's diet, tea and toast
(How old is he? Ninety-four?),
He can go to sleep in sagging
Age and wake as Roger Moore,

Only in his dossier
Rotting like a Dorian Gray.
Leave the balcony unlocked
And he'll slip out for days and days,

Where he's gone top secret, always,
Never one Wish You Were Here.
He recalls them by their perfumes,
Names them, like champagnes, by year.

3. *Hymn to Sean Connery*

Connery, how did I end up
A double o thirty-year-old
Father of two?

So must all international adolescents of mystery
Grow into men domestically mastered—

For the hand that begins as a Walther PPK,
Knuckles by the cheek, index finger in the air,
Ages into a handshake
And signs, signs, signs away,

And time that strolls past the daydreaming
Camera shutter
Has been known to turn without warning
And with the gun hidden at its side
Shoot daydreamers dead,

The circle swaying to and fro
Before it tumbles to the lower right-hand corner,
Goes white, and dilates
Into the first scene
Of the rest of a life.

Connery, before the baccarat, you, too,
Held earthly burdens, earthly offices—
Bricklayer, coffin polisher, milkman;

Connery, eternal bachelor, may I, too,
Someday unzip this mortal scuba suit
And reveal the tuxedo beneath.

Notice the face of the Infant, the deep-set
      eyes, the sharpness of the nose.
His body is tallow, his face is stone.
      The dissonance is Photoshop.
Not one of the Kings, not the lamb, not the Virgin—
      only the Infant in this scene
is staring the camera down, so to speak,
      observing us observing him.
We know that the Master could show, when he wished to,
      a youthful softness—witness his
Madonna and Clouds, his *Persephone,*
      both paintings dated 1515,
the same year as this one. The Virgin herself
      is much more childlike than her child.
That gaze is deliberately worldly-wise,
      or maybe otherworldly-wise.
To its left, on loan from the Prado, you see
      Self-Portrait with a Tongue of Fire,
which the Master completed the year of his fall
      from Barcelona's cathedral scaffold.
The titular "tongue" is the paintbrush with which
      he paints himself as on a mirror—
with fractures to both of his arms, he was forced
      to clip the brush between his teeth.
Foreshortened, it's roughly the length of a tongue,
      emerging from the bitter smile
of an archangel smitten for heady ambition.
      He soon preferred his handicap

to his hands; he never did go back.

I had to lick myself onto

the canvas, he wrote to a friend years later,

like polish off the boots of God—

So now you're mouthing off to God, too?
The voice He gave me's too strong not to.

FUGITO ERGO SUM.
The escaped slave's motto.

Get down on your knees and do it.
Slowly. The way you were taught to.

Mine eyes have seen the glory
As they damn well ought to.

An eye for an eye won't sate Him.
Good thing I brought two.

a. NEUROSCIENCE

What used to be illusory
Is measured now in real mists
Of neurochemicals

Nothing neural is chimerical

The "Mind" is nothing, while the Brain
Is nothing if not realist

Assaying with a fine-tuned spine
Its parts per million of pain

(And skeptical of love or poem
Until precise receptors hum)

It turns out Marx was right, a hymn's
A little hit of heroin

The Lord, the Lord is IV morphine

The Devil is in the endorphins

b. ERASURE OF THE FINAL SCENE OF *KING LEAR* (1)

Take away meaning.
Kneel and ask of rogues
the mystery of things.
Fire eyes flesh: Come hither.

Question the old and miserable
Father power. Stand up.
No prophets should we stomach.
Prisoners, witness, I create my lord.

Joy lies in blood, bread,
art, medicine.
His name, name, name is lost.
Bare-gnawn noble speech,

honour this toad-spotted heart.
Warlike tongue,
spurn, bruise, speak!
The law is paper.

The law cannot govern
the dark place of sweetness.
Rags and stones
reveal this blessing,

a flawed joy, but not
a bell that rings for the slave.
Bodies, alive, atremble, touch us
with urges poisoned and brief:

Time is a stain, a plague,
a cross deserving
a dog, a horse, a rat.
Never, never, never button your lips:

Wonder has usurped his soul rule.

The journey calls.

We must obey what we feel.

So *march*.

b.   ERASURE OF THE FINAL SCENE OF *KING LEAR* (II)

Birds, butterflies, foxes

thrive in my bosom.

I sweat and bleed

and feel their sharpness.

Father, brother, husband,

sister, wife:

Love all in my name.

Sickness is before you.

I come.

I place below thy foot

my heart.

Wisdom should breathe and bruise.

I answer you

with my son.

I am here, nursing death,

blessing from first to last

the clamour and the pity

and the howl, howl, howl.

Here on the cross

I am desperately present.

Look up.

a. RADIOLOGY

Picture the fibrous spokewheel-
scaffold of an infinitely thin
wafer of orange

held to a window, transilluminated
in its circumference of rind.
Now picture a volume of human

reduced to planes and fluttering
under my thumb like a flip-book
showing the disease in action.

Every one of those planes: hundreds of lines
stacked tight enough to resolve
the speck not yet a lump.

Every one of those lines: a string
of pixels end to end, razor-
luminous horizon round a darkening world.

Each pixel: a point geometry
defines dimensionless, no height,
no width, no death. I see what ails the body

by regressing body back to spirit:
the volume a stack of planes, the plane a row
of lines, the line a string of points,

and the point, at last, nothing at all, all form
substanceless by radiologic proof. I read
no images more imaginary than

the mind's, every layer of it immaterial—
the gray matter,
the white matter,

the dark.

C.   STEM CELLS

In the hospital's hothouse,
cardiac strawberries blink on a vine.
A walnut shell hides a brain rich
in good fat; a lychee's peel,
a pale eyeball high in vitamin C.
The doctor has good news!
His pharmacopoeia has given way
to a cornucopia,
one that spills ovarian grapes
and bananas that promise never to go soft.
A single stem has borne, has birthed fruit
that shall not be forbidden us.
The pomegranate spleen, yea,
the kidney-bean kidney shall be ours.

Splendid! delights a voice
over the hospital PA system.
Splendid, you summer-sweet sons of Adam—
using an apple seed of Knowledge
to grow the Tree of Life!

No one can say whose voice it is,
but its hiss is a scythe's.

d.   HERETICAL FUGUE

That Christ
did not always exist but was created
by, and subordinate to, the Father.

That the Father
and his Son are shoot and cutting, Christ
at the moment of severance created.

That the created
Christ was distinct from the true Christ
as the living God is from your dying father.

That Christ,
by being born of a virgin, created
a rival cult of the Mother.

That the Mother
is always indulgent, the Father
always angry toward the life they created.

That the Father
tortured the Son in front of his Mother
until she wailed *please stop for the love of Christ—*

I just couldn't breathe in its shadow.
It weighed what the cross weighed, that shadow
Cross, more than any shadow should. No
Sun could shoulder that kind of shadow,
No man kneel there without a shudder.
The dark beams crushed me flat as shadow,
My flesh, grass, matted by the shade. No
Way a mere cedar cross could shed so
Much dark matter, so weighty a shadow.
I just couldn't breathe in that shadow
Until I made myself a shadow-
Swallowing sea and swallowed shadow

The way a sea will swallow daylight.
The shadow splashed down, and the sun's light
Spilled over—only I was the light's
Sole source, both the prism and the light
Beam split into the eye's wide palette.
The splash displaced a volume of light
Equal to one sun, this light the light
That made of the shadow-cross a light
Cross to bear, the light that raised my light-
Weight body until then strange to flight

But now, death made light of by his dying,
Light-footed, fallen, risen, flying.

Virus infinitely versatile. Virus
Of guardrail, iPod, turnstile. Virus

Eager to go
The extra mile. Virus

Seaborne, colonizing
The Enchanted Isles. Virus

Airborne, whistling
All the while. Virus

Discreetly flashing holster
And assassin smile. Virus

Smuggling fever up
The Red Nile. Virus

Of folk song, urban legend,
Official denial. Virus

Squatting on the sky
Chameleon-style. Virus

In New York City scheming
How to make a pile. Virus

Never standing
Trial. Virus

Believing God
Gave it guile. Virus

Making a killing and
Making it in style.

e.   THE WALTZ OF DESCARTES AND MOHAMMED

There is
No God
But God.
I think
Therefore
I am.

I am;
There is
Therefore
No God.
I think,
"But God,

But *God* . . ."
I am,
I . . . think.
Is there
No *God*
Therefore?

Therefore
Good for
No God

Am I.
There is,
I think,

"I." Think
There: For
There is
But God.
I am
No God,

No good.
I think
I am
Here but
For God.
There is . . .

I think there is
No God but the God
I am there for.

f.   FE

Translate chemistry into Spanish, and iron
is faith—this pile of shavings,
the Devil's own toenails, the same
ore that's at our origin, heme.
Of all the metals, the ferrous to me seems
fairest. Aurum is more ardent, argent
rarer, but blood's core ore, though everywhere,
is precious air. I prefer

meteoric iron, pig iron, iron wrought or rust

(its every red felicitous for us)

to fetid sulfur and the fey ironies

of faded faith. Without heme's boxcars, our

carbon would oxygen-starve, without heme's

hexagon, the only Ferris wheel

air cares to ride. Breath's effort otherwise

would be nothing for, sigh after sigh heaved

through a sieve. Hymn heme,

this matter of life and breath, using the very

inspiration it is carrying. Hymn heme

for carrying us home,

in the femoral Styx, in the infernal vein

this iron oar of the Ferryman.

g.   HOLY

The firefly sees a knife twist in the lid of the jar

and thinks: *Okay, at least this kid is going to give me stars.*

The stars will tell you, even emptiness has pores—her black

holes open by the thousand when she sprawls and suns her back.

Our one-way ears, the face's clustered input/output jacks—

just block the ports that hook us up, and watch the screens go black.

The eyes are mine shafts, and dripping they lead down to the mind

whose diamonds tip our heaven-drills. Evolving or designed,

this holeyness is all the evidence of God we get,

that and the patient rain of showerhead on shower grate

whose local summer says, *Step in and open up your mouth,*

says *Drink and sing!* because what's out wants in, what's in wants out.

It's why we cut windows in any place we mean to live—

the airtight suffocates us. We survive by being sieves.

Spermaceti, blowholes gouged by the Lord God's harpoon,
sing in their ice-cap chapels, *Blessed is the breathing wound.*

g. DEVOLUTION

Pink, filigreed, whimsically intricate
At ear and iris, man marked

The pinnacle of God's rococo period.
Showy technique tricked out that late art—

No more the high geometry of angels,
Those perfect freehand circles, lines, and angles.

Man had been veined labyrinthine, studded
With senses, jointed with balls, sockets, hinges.

His mind was a jungle of nerves, his skin
All marshy with sweat glands—an omnium-

Gatherum of naked, downy, hairy; squishy,
Knobby, slippery, pimply; round, sloped, flat.

The Master, grown sick of his own slick skill,
Longed for heart and the heart's simplicity

That made the sun and the other stars.
And so he started to unstack

The odd fantastic shapes
Of vertebrae, unwire

The self-indulgently
Complex cerebral cortex,

Reroute the circulation
Into a sloshing trough,

His specious species rinsed
Of its once-precious reason.

That knotty body
Was soon streamlined

Into a flatworm
Devoid of eyes,

From that into
A sessile sponge,

A passive hollow
Instead of lungs,

The all too clever
Device revised

To a divine
Simplicity

That the Lord
God loved well:

Amoeboid
Believer,

One Monk
In one

Cell.

f.   "THERE FELL A GREAT STAR"

Their shadows flickered and stretched to the west.
The future fixed its lidless eye
On concrete switchgrass, furrows of asphalt.
Telescopes, searchlights aimed on high
Shot the flare of the mind at darkness.
We stood on the moon but failed to scry
The star called wormwood.

The signal changed, but the curbs stayed full
Though seconds before the world was spinning.
Why shouldn't a light announce the end
When light alone pronounced the beginning?
Men in nooses of patterned satin
Welcomed this end to wanting and winning,
This star called wormwood.

The women who stood on pencil heels,
The cubicle drones of the moneycomb
Were tired of sugar, tired of gold.
They looked to the blaze as a blessed home.
This star was a mercy, this Stella Maris
That sheltered them in its fusion dome,
This star called wormwood.

We raise our arms against the rain
And find the lines on our palms erased.
The dew is puddle-gray and bitter,
But we learn to love the aftertaste
Here where loosestrife meadows the square
And flash-blind featherless sparrows praise
The star called wormwood.

e.   HIDE AND SEEK

I am
that I
am. It
is what
it is.
So there.

You're wishing there
were an *I am*
in all that is,
wishing that I
lived inside what
I've made—this lit

and artless, heart-lit
world like no other,
bejouled. Light is what
I spoke, not where I am.
I like my space. I
like space. Though space is

not exactly spacious
for someone infinite,
I, my uppercase I,
can stand at full height there.
Ego is all I am—
scrawny letter, lots of weight.

From ether to the earthy wheat
I stretch a sunlit isthmus,
my being, my burning *I am*
a star forever beyond its
own shining. I am, in theory,
pure subjectivity, an I

that cons, conjures, conjugates as *I*
am, I shall smite, I created it—
call it experimental theater,
a one-man show whose star your eyes miss
no matter where in the house you sit.
I disappear in my role. I am

most myself when I am where absence is.
Blue unreal irises, what is it
you think you see? Look away. There I am.

Out on the Limpopo
with a hoopoe for a top hat
steps a hippopotamus
improbably debonair,

his once-hapless heft
supple enough at the hoof
to play a Gymnopédie
on crocodile keys.

He's given up
his low mopes
in bottomless mud
for rose pips and flip plovers.

A philosopher-hippo,
as it happens,
harbors a libido
hopelessly Augustinian. So

now, nicely evolved
from hypocrisy
to apostasy
to hippopotamus,

he's off to a hip
Limpopo dive,
its happening scene,
its happy shallows.

In the first crate
he crowbars open:
Veteran Enfields
on a bed of

shredded paper,
four in a row,
a quatrain-tidy
Armageddon.

In the second:
Belts for a Maxim
gun's spondaic
hellhole elegy.

Like Prometheus,
smuggling fire.
Like Prometheus
by the shrill call

by the scalpel
of an eagle
baited, gutted,
bayoneted.

Here in Harar
he hardly ever
hears the fever
still malarial

in his bloodstream,
music itching
out of reach in
his mind's ear.

Coffee prices,
shipping schedules
drown his ear in
interference.

French, that purebred,
hounds him down a
willful Abyss-
inian deafness

where he flees that
Sorbonne-sordid
anguish language:
Racine, rapine,

Chateaubrigand,
Verlaine in chains.
Listen: his third crate
is the word crate

of his smuggler's
number-nimble
skull: the bootleg
plosives laid in

line-break fuses,
lit and loaded.

A single sonnet
and the whole

Pléiade exploded.

The beauty sleeps
Guarded by a leopard
In the witch's garden
Under an apple tree.

The apple tree
In the garden guards
A beautiful leopard
From the witchcraft of sleep.

The leopard whisks
The beauty out of the garden
After a treated apple
Leaves the guards asleep.

The beauty wishes
Under an apple tree
For her guardian to sleep
So she can leap the garden wall.

The garden-variety witch
Who slept with the leopard
Under the apple tree
Wakes up beautiful.

On her guard in the garden,
The apple-cheeked beauty
Bewitches the leopard
Moments before his leap.

No one guarded the apple tree
And now, awakened beauty
Prowls the garden
In a leopard print dress.

He launched his body's burnished bone spears
  beyond the race to a point beyond despair,
    what broke in him, broken open, like a spore.

Prior to everything but pang and prayer,
  he watches us inside a stillness freer
    than all the speed that harries us through the air.

His mind unknowable, his face unknown,
  the part that lasts was in between them: Bones
    that die hard let us know him for our own.

His rise is a promise we will not go under
  the jackhammer rain or river's power sander
    but take more killing than a death can render

because we are the pearl and pit of matter,
  infinite mind in a rind of dura mater
    the hardest thing that matter ever mothered,

our historiography of wounds
  graven deeper than the flighty winds
    that make a rubbing of our eloquence.

Life likes a little mess. All patterns need a snarl.
The best patterns know how best to heed a snarl.

Every high style, every strict form was once nonce.
The best way to save a snagged pattern? Repeat the snarl.

Eden used to snow in fractals, rain in syncopated runs.
Adam never imagined he would hear its seedlings snarl.

Tug the wrong thread, and your wool sweater vanishes at once.
Death pulls at a wisp of us—and just like that, it's freed the snarl.

What *is* it about order that we love? This sense,
Maybe, that a secret informs the pattern?

Is it a toddler's joy in doing things again?
Is it the entropy in us that warms to pattern?

I never intended this line to rhyme on *again* again.
Then again, sometimes it's the snarl that adorns the pattern.

Ab ovo

    or from supernova,

    we're less *de novo* than

abracadabra,

    materializing

    like the magician's

rabbits

    copulating, populating

    the top hat.

Aborigines

    hopscotched by oar stroke

    isle to isle:

Absolute

    originality, the sort

    that antedates granddaddy

Abraham's,

    always hides

    a Polynesian canoe,

Babylonian

    potsherd,

    or swiftly defrosting

able-

        bodied Siberian
        sealskin hunter.

A birth

        certificate is an erasure
        made from

obits:

        We first emerge, we emerge
        first from a belly-deep

abyss

        and bawl
        a waterlogged

aubade.

        Behind that beginning?
        An egg, a sperm. An

absence.

The arms I sing. Forget the man, there is
no other epic. Sing the arms of kids,
the ones with pustules all along their veins

like runway track lights burning for a plane
that blew up hours ago with no survivors.
The ones with runes no parent can decipher,

one message, knifed and scarred and knifed again
in a mystic tongue forgotten who knows when.
The arms imprinted with a shadow grip

as if the dad who grabbed and crushed had dipped
his hand in black paint first. The arms with tight
arcs of perforation: human bites

that get infected faster than a dog's.
The toddler's arms with both hands scalded raw
all glisteny and hog-pink, swollen taut,

the tantrum over, the lesson taught,
two signal fires that call across a plain
the city is sacked and all the children slain.

ACKNOWLEDGMENTS

The author wishes to thank the editors of the following publications, in which these poems first appeared:

AGNI online: "Are You Hungry?," "The Enduring Appeal of the Western Canon" (nominated for the Pushcart Prize)

America: "There Fell a Great Star"

American Arts Quarterly: "In a Gallery" (nominated for the Pushcart Prize)

Asheville Poetry Review: the two erasures from the final scene of *King Lear* (under the titles "Agon Embedded in the Final Scene of *King Lear* [I]" and "Agon Embedded in the Final Scene of *King Lear* [II]")

The Atlantic: "The Interrogation" and "Dynasty" (under the title "Lineage")

The Awl: "The Star-Spangled Turban"

The Best American Poetry 2012: "The Autobiography of Khwaja Mustasim"

The Best of the Best American Poetry 25th Anniversary Edition: "The Autobiography of Khwaja Mustasim"

Best of the Net 2012: "His Love of Semicolons"

Cimarron Review: "The Metamorphosis"

The Dark Horse (UK): "The Boy Who Couldn't Grow Up" and "Augustine the Hippo"

Drunken Boat: "Pandemic Ghazal" (nominated for the Pushcart Prize)

The Economy: "Heretical Fugue" and "Crocodile Porn"

E-Verse Radio: "James Bond Suite"

Field: A Journal of Poetry and Poetics: "Radiology" (under the title "Day Job"), "Ode to a Drone," and "Welcome Home, Troops!"

The Hairpin: "Save the Candor"

The Hampden-Sydney Poetry Review: "Holy"

Harvard Divinity Bulletin: "Fe"

IMAGE: "The Waltz of Descartes and Mohammed" and "Shadow-Cross Fugue"

Kenyon Review online: "Steep Ascension" (as part of a memorial for the poet John Hollander) and "1914: The Name Game" (on the 100th anniversary of the outbreak of World War I)

Linebreak: "James Bond Suite"

The New Criterion: "The Top" and "Winged Words"

The New Republic: "Sex" and "The Illuminator"

The New Yorker: "The Autobiography of Khwaja Mustasim," "Dothead," "T.S.A.," "To the Hyphenated Poets," and "Invocation"

The New York Review of Books: "Immigration and Naturalization" and "Neuroscience"

The Norton Introduction to Literature, eleventh edition: "Dothead"

Old Flame: From the First 10 Years of 32 Poems Magazine: "Taste Bud Sonzal"

The Paris-American: "Love Song for Doomed Youth"

Plume: "Abecedarian," "Joint Effort," and "Hide and Seek"

Poetry: "Horse Apocalypse" and "Save the Candor"

Poetry Northwest: "Devolution" and "Rimbaud in Harar"

Prairie Schooner: "To Anne Sexton"

River Styx: "The Doll"

Smithsonian: "Pattern and Snarl," "Black Hands," "Kennewick Man Elegy," and "Stem Cells"

Think Journal: "Dystopiary"

32 Poems: "Rune Poem," "Et Tu," "Training Course," "Taste Bud Sonzal," "Recombinant Fairy Tale," and "From the Egg"

Tin House online: "Killshot"

Umbrella: "His Love of Semicolons"

Virginia Quarterly Review: "Lineage"

The epigraphic image on page vi reproduces a page from *Hobson-Jobson: A Glossary of Colloquial Anglo-Indian Words and Phrases, and of Kindred Terms, Etymological, Historical, Geographical and Discursive,* compiled by Henry Yule and Arthur C. Burnell in 1886.

A NOTE ABOUT THE AUTHOR

Amit Majmudar is a diagnostic nuclear radiologist who lives in Dublin, Ohio, with his wife, twin sons, and baby daughter. His poetry and prose have appeared in *The New York Times, The New Yorker, The Atlantic, The Best American Poetry* (2007, 2012), *The Best of the Best American Poetry 1988–2012, Poetry, Poetry Daily,* and several other venues, including the eleventh edition of *The Norton Introduction to Literature.* His first poetry collection, *0°, 0°,* was released by Northwestern University Press/Triquarterly Books in 2009 and was a finalist for the Poetry Society of America's Norma Farber First Book Award. His second poetry collection, *Heaven and Earth,* won the 2011 Donald Justice Prize. He blogs for *Kenyon Review* and is also a critically acclaimed novelist.

A NOTE ON THE TYPE

This book was set in Scala, a typeface designed by the Dutch designer
Martin Majoor (b. 1960) in 1988 and released by the FontFont foundry in
1990. While designed as a fully modern family of fonts containing both a
serif and a sans serif alphabet, Scala retains many refinements normally
associated with traditional fonts.

Composed by North Market Street Graphics,
Lancaster, Pennsylvania

Printed and bound by Berryville Graphics,
Berryville, Virginia

Designed by Soonyoung Kwon